CW01307162

Copyright © 2024

Written and illustrated by Samantha Finn and Hannah Whelan

All rights reserved. No part of this book may be reproduced or used in any manner without the prior written permission of the copyright owner, except for the use of brief quotations in a book review.

CHICO GOES BACK IN TIME

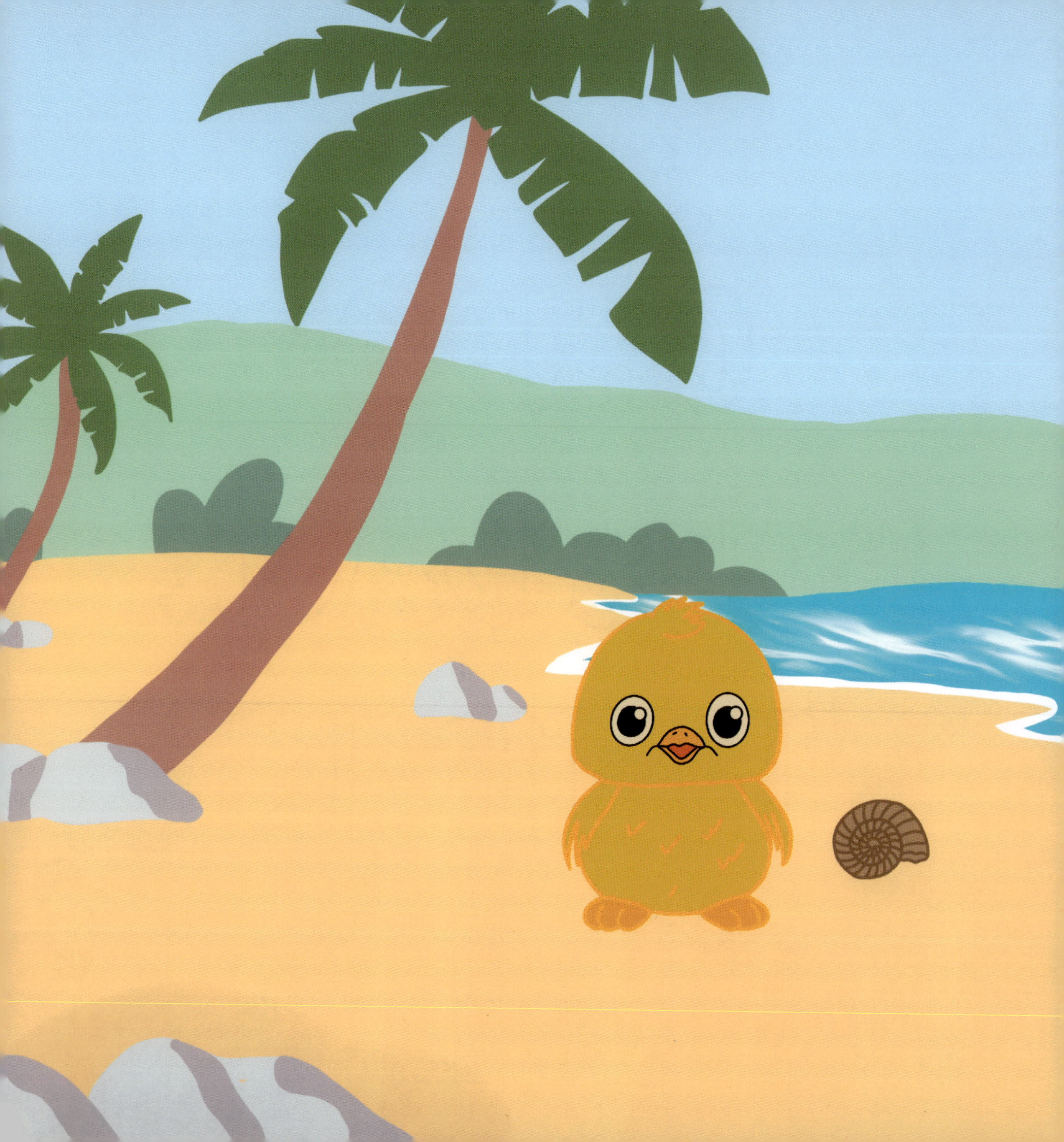

One day Chico was at the beach, when he noticed a funny looking rock sticking out of the sand.

Chico was looking at the funny rock, when suddenly a little smiley snail appeared.

Sally the snail smiled up at Chico and said 'That's a fossil from a long, long time ago'.

'A time when dinosaurs were around?', asked Chico.

'Yes, I can take you back in time to introduce you to some of my dinosaur friends if you would like?' asked Sally.

Chico jumped at the adventure to go back in time with Sally to learn more about dinosaurs.

And so, as they flew through time, Chico wondered who he was about to meet.

Once they made it back in time, Chico was surprised! Everywhere looked so different!

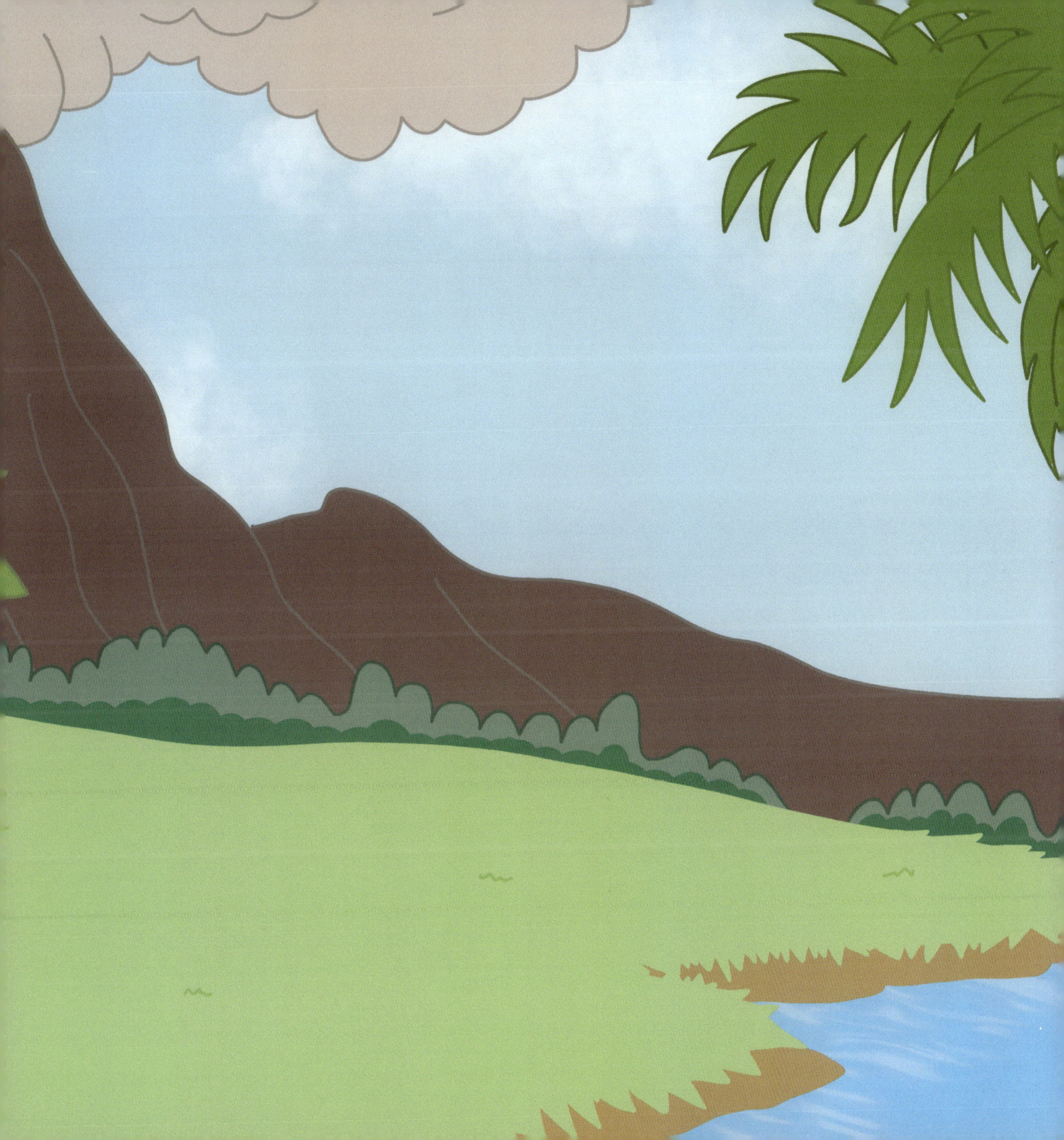

All of a sudden, Chico heard a loud squawking.

'What was that?', asked Chico nervously.

Sally explained that some dinosaurs could fly high in the sky, 'That one there is Pete, he is the fastest flyer!, shouted Sally over the loud sounds.

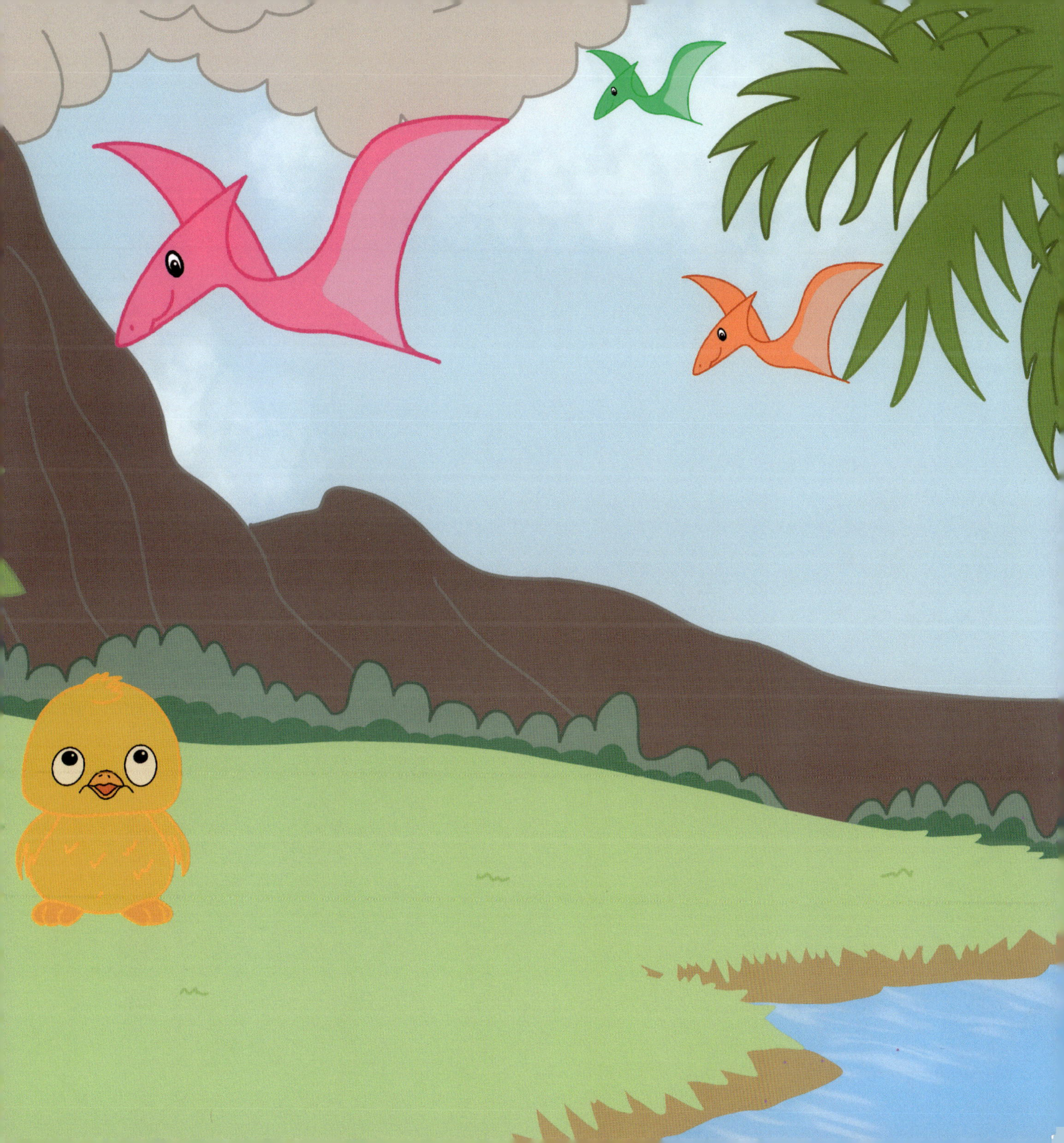

Chico was so focused on Pete and his friends flying around when he noticed the very big dinosaur behind them.

'Sally, stay very still, there is a big dinosaur behind you!', whispered Chico

'Excuse me, I notice you are standing under this yummy tree, do you mind if I have a quick snack', asked the big dinosaur so politely.

'Oh, I'm sorry Mr Dinosaur. Do you always eat trees?' asked Chico.

'Yes, I only eat the plants around here and this tree is my favourite snack!', explained the dinosaur.

'Be careful though, not all dinosaurs only eat plants!', he explained.

'We will leave you to eat your snack', Chico and Sally said as they thanked the dinosaur for his advice and set off to explore more.

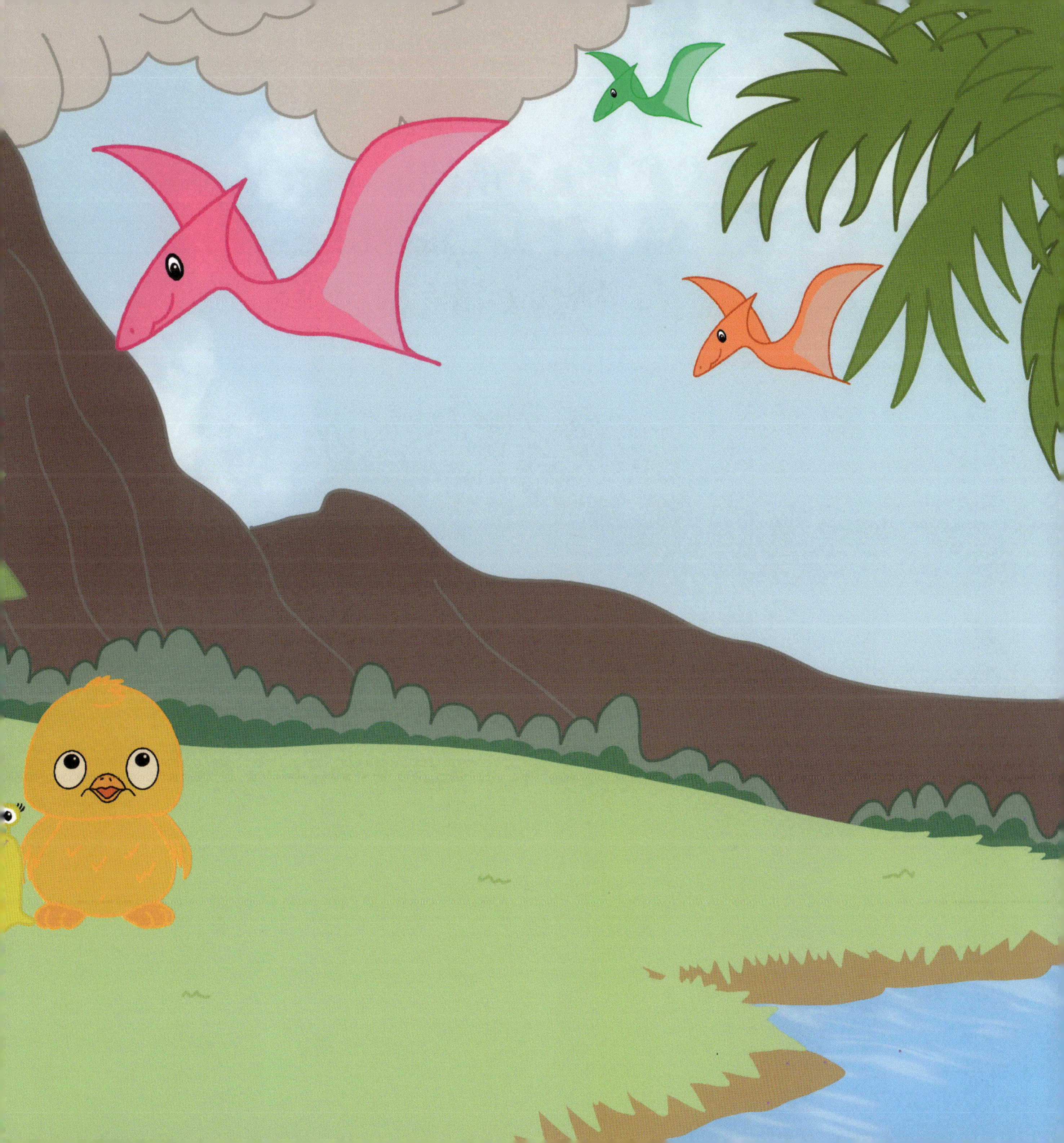

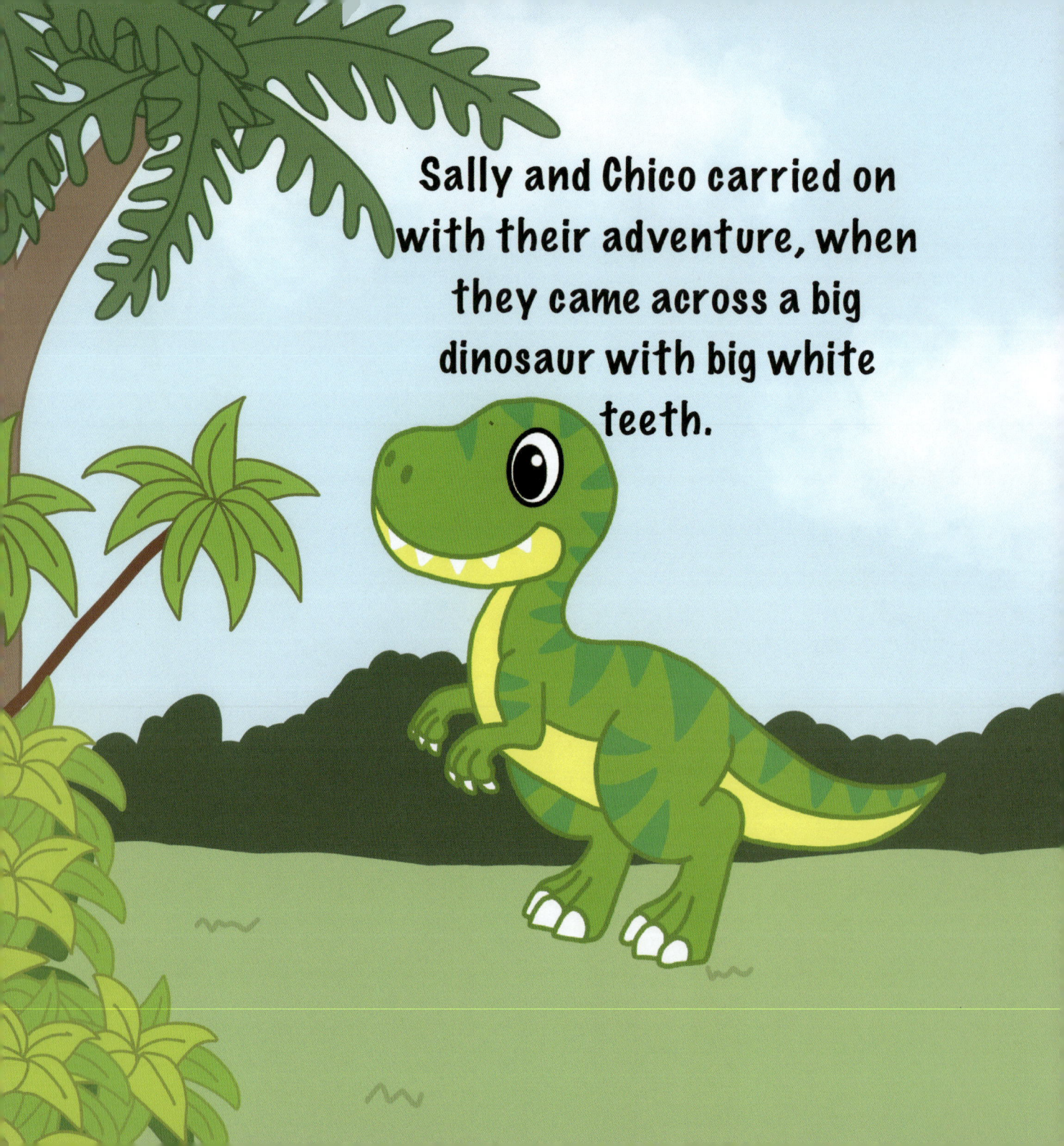

Sally and Chico carried on with their adventure, when they came across a big dinosaur with big white teeth.

'You need to stay quiet, that's a T-Rex, we don't want to scare him', whispered Sally

Suddenly, the T-Rex turned around and spotted Sally and Chico by the bushes.

'Well hello there little one, my name is Tony, I haven't seen you around here before', said Tony.

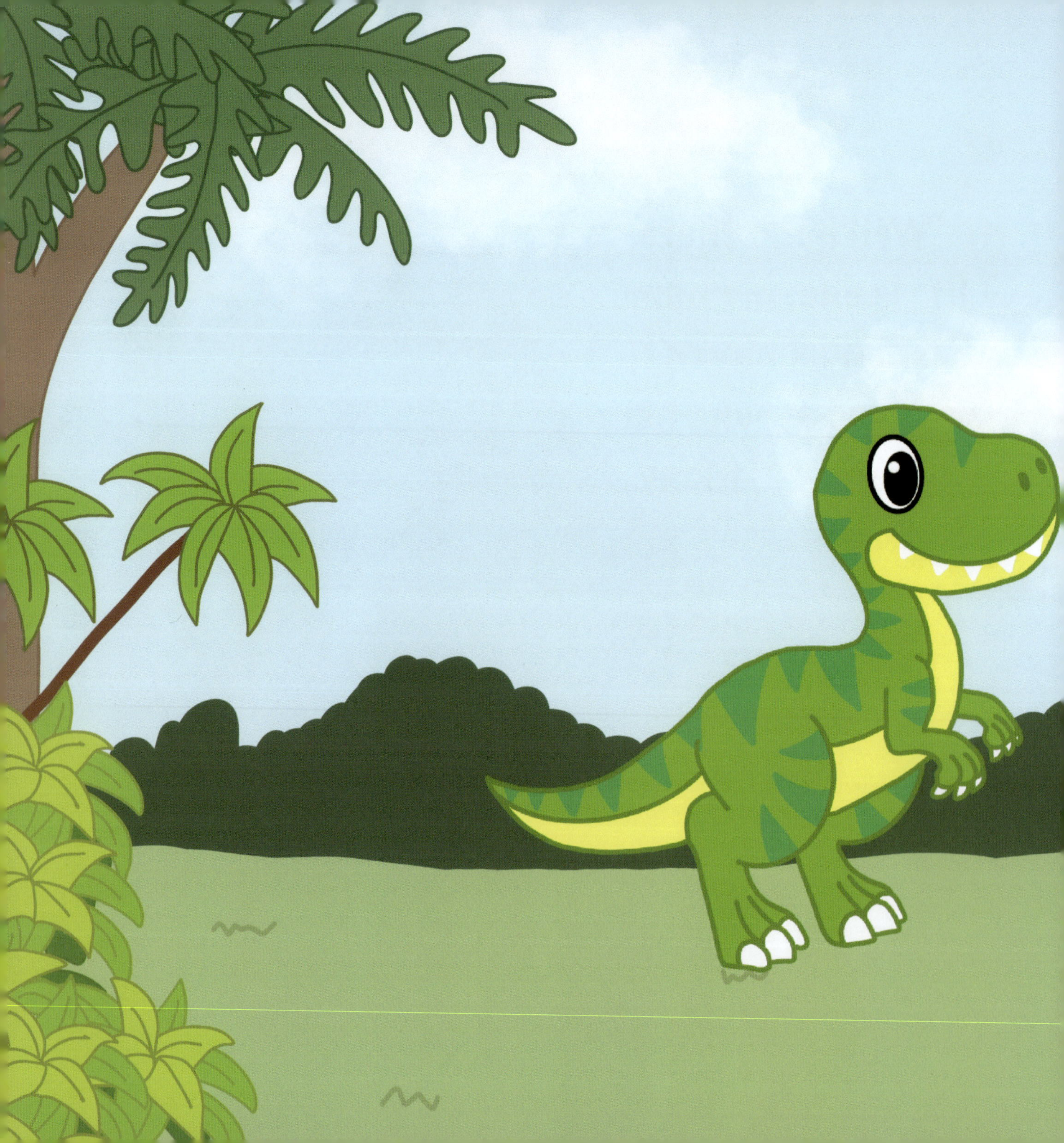

'I-I'm just visiting, I want to learn about dinosaurs', said Chico nervously.

'Well you are in the right place, there are all kinds of dinosaurs stomping around here', laughed Tony.

'I am late for lunch with my mama so I wish you luck on your adventure', said Tony as he set off home.

'Do you hear that?' asked Sally looking, 'It sounds like thunder'.

'Let's go and find out where it is coming from!', said Chico.

Chico and Sally came across an open field, the ground was shaking and the sound of stomping filled the air.

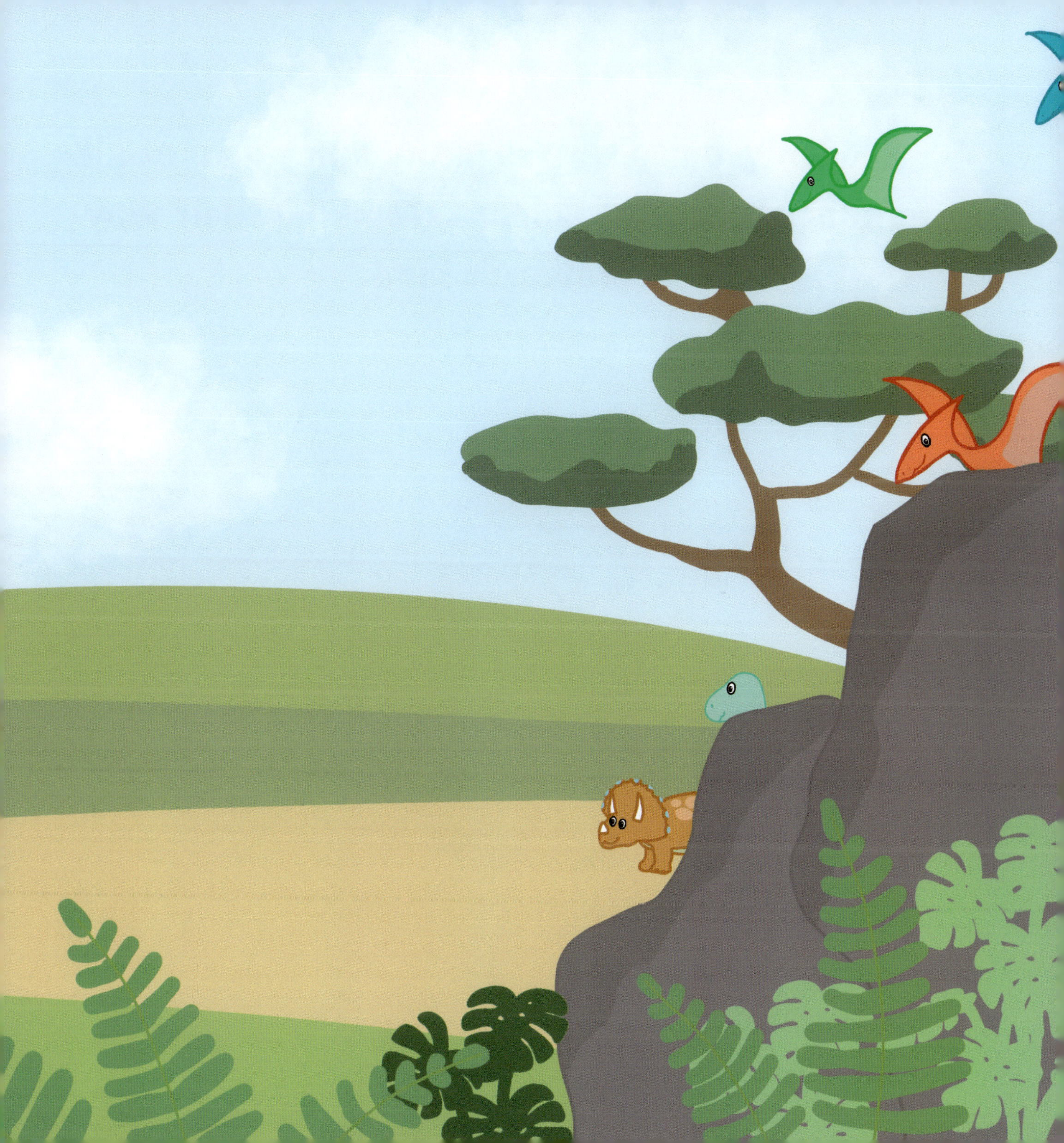

Suddenly, Chico saw so many dinosaurs, of all shapes, sizes and colours stomping their way towards him!

They are all look so magical!

'It's a stampeed!', yelled Sally over the loud stomping, 'We had better get home before we get hurt!'.

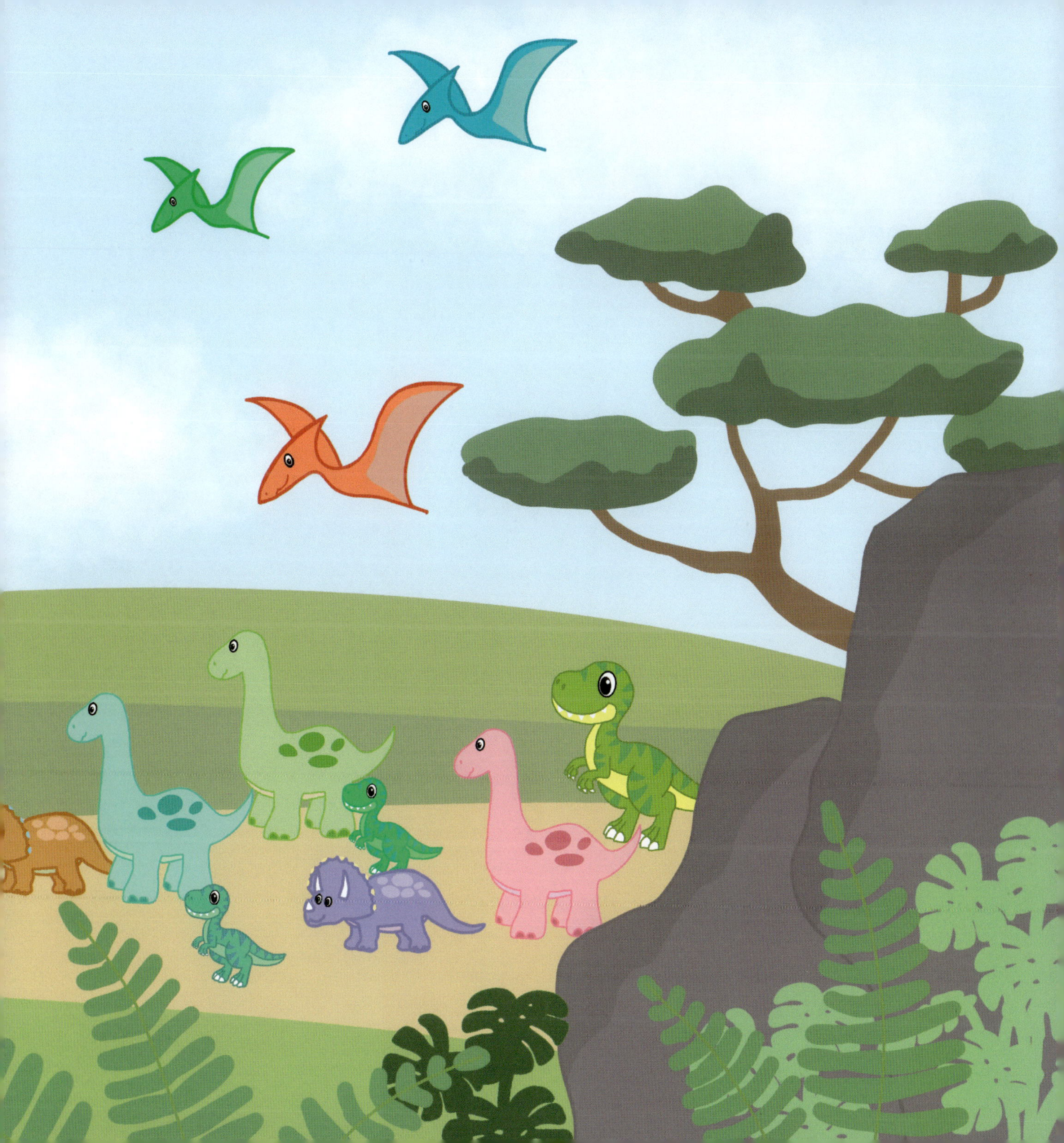

Chico was sad that the adventure had come to an end, but he knew it was time to travel back to his time in the future.

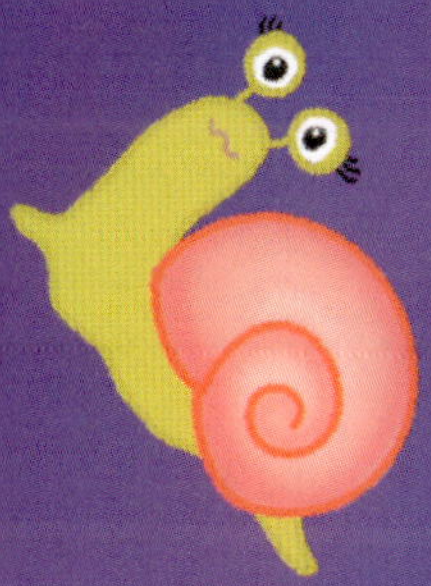

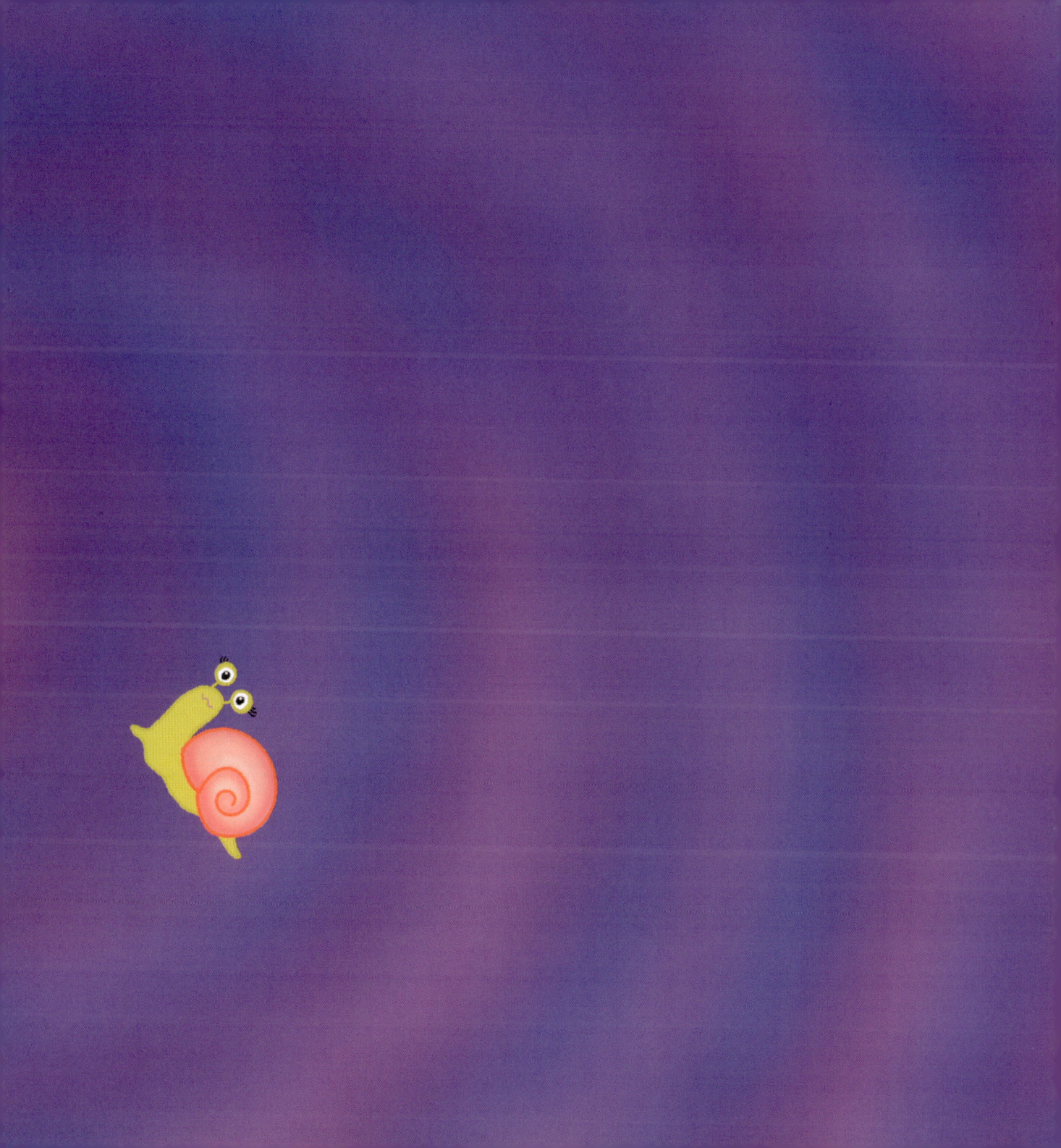

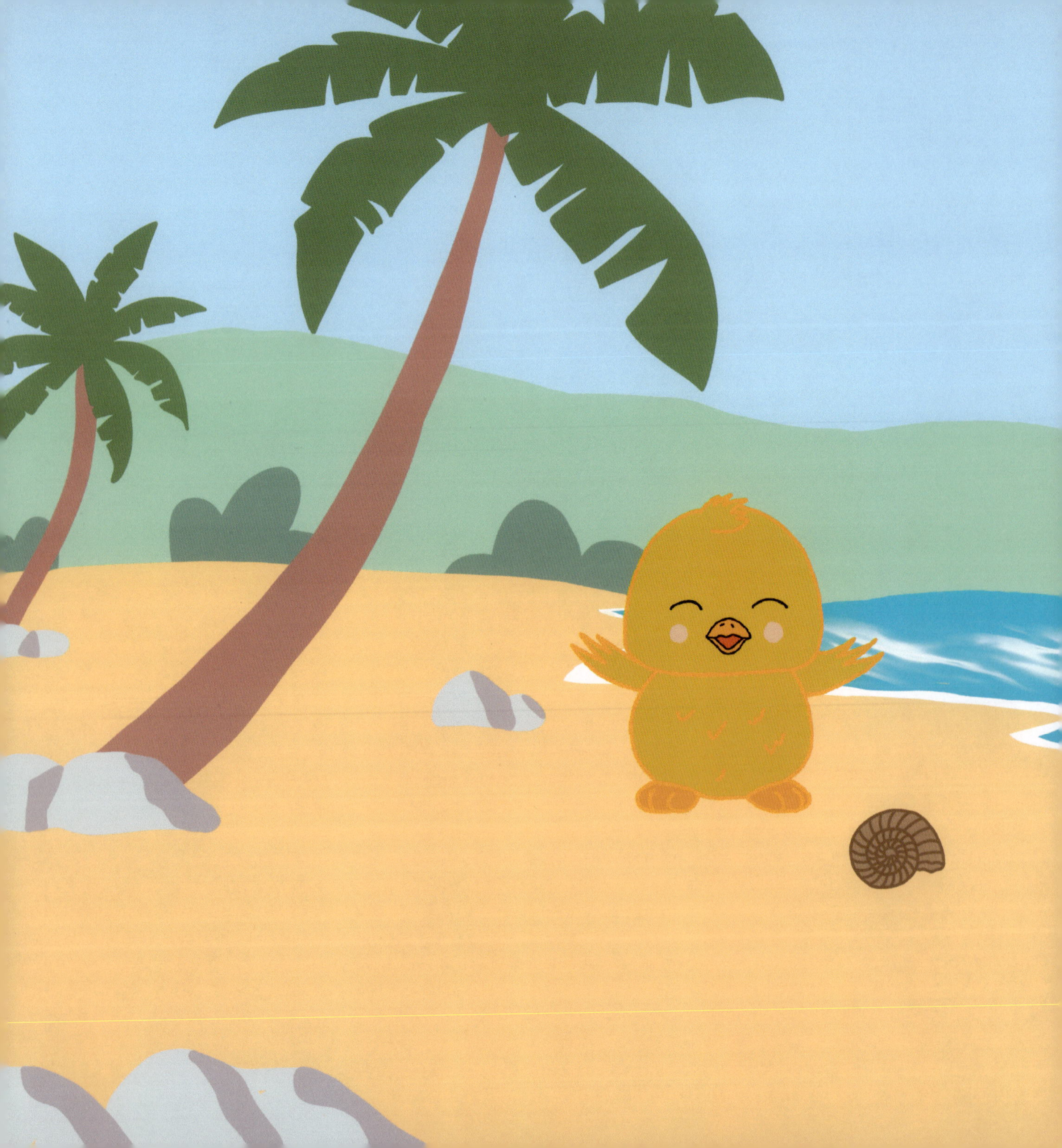

Once they arrived back safely on the beach, Chico realised what an amazing adventure he had just been on!

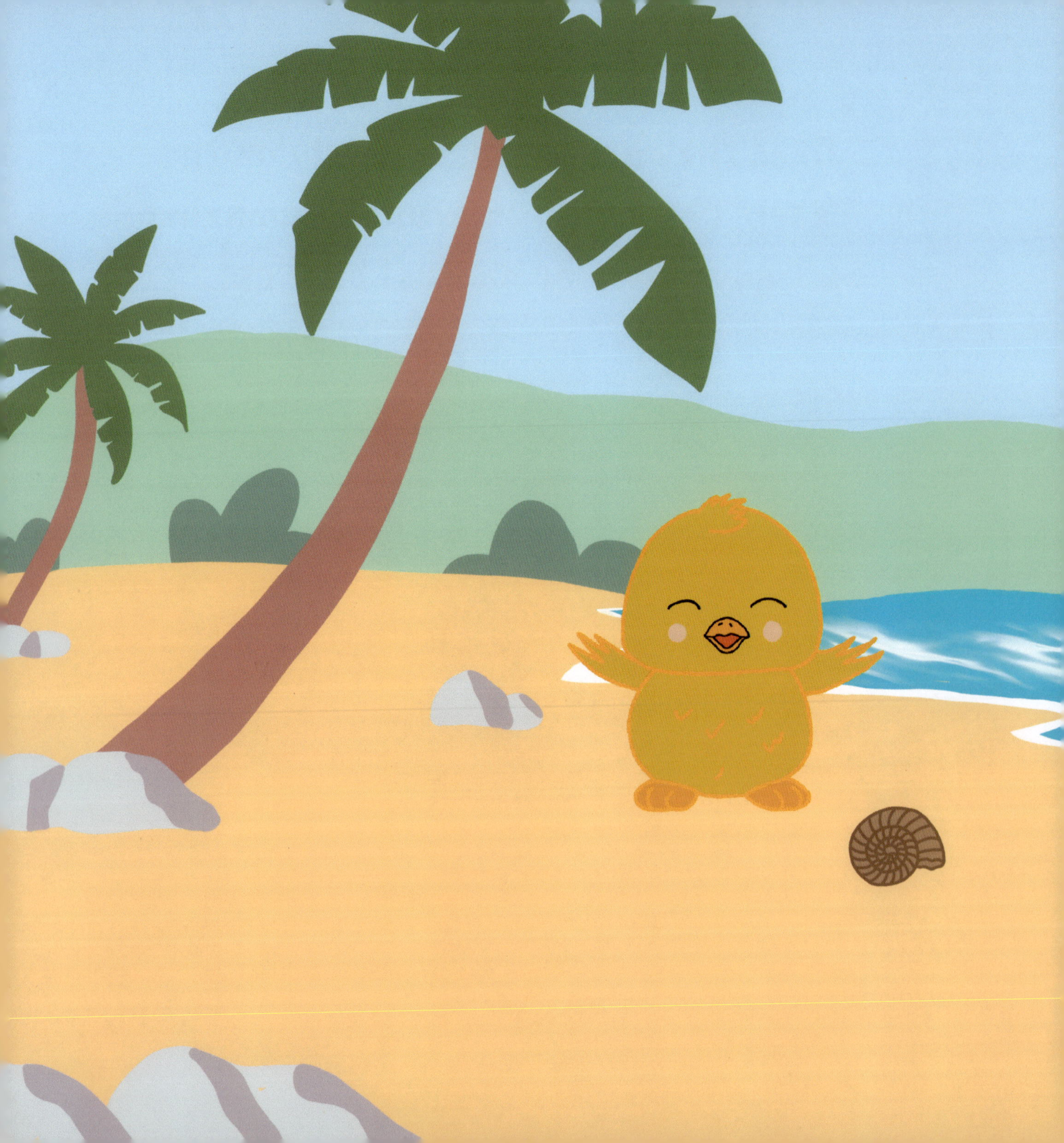

'Not many chicks can say they have a T-Rex friend!', laughed Chico as he thanked Sally for taking him back in time.

I wonder what Chico will get up to next...

Printed in Great Britain
by Amazon